Scales, Riffs & Solos
you can learn today!

▶▶ *FastForward*™
Guitar
Scales
with Rikky Rooksby

D1388865

Wise Publications
London / New York / Sydney / Paris / Copenhagen / Madrid / Tokyo

Exclusive Distributors:
Music Sales Limited
8/9 Frith Street, London W1D 3JB, England.
Music Sales Pty Limited
120 Rothschild Avenue, Rosebery, NSW 2018, Australia.
Music Sales Corporation
257 Park Avenue South, New York, NY10010,
United States of America.

Order No.AM963710
ISBN 0-7119-8130-2
This book © Copyright 2001 by Wise Publications.

Written and arranged by Rikky Rooksby.
Edited by Sorcha Armstrong.
Music processed by Paul Ewers Music Design.
Cover Photograph (PRS Private Stock #62, McCarty hollowbody
with one-piece maple top) courtesy of Outline Press.
Artist photographs courtesy of LFI and Redferns.

Printed and bound in the United Kingdom.

Your Guarantee of Quality:
As publishers, we strive to produce every book to
the highest commercial standards.
The music has been freshly engraved and the book has
been carefully designed to minimise awkward page turns
and to make playing from it a real pleasure.
Particular care has been given to specifying acid-free,
neutral-sized paper made from pulps which have not
been elemental chlorine bleached.
This pulp is from farmed sustainable forests and
was produced with special regard for the environment.
Throughout, the printing and binding have
been planned to ensure a sturdy, attractive publication
which should give years of enjoyment.
If your copy fails to meet our high standards, please
inform us and we will gladly replace it.

Music Sales' complete catalogue describes
thousands of titles and is available in full colour sections
by subject, direct from Music Sales Limited.
Please state your areas of interest and send a cheque/postal
order for £1.50 for postage to: Music Sales Limited,
Newmarket Road, Bury St. Edmunds, Suffolk IP33 3YB.

www.musicsales.com

Guitar Tablature Explained

Guitar music can be notated three different ways: on a musical stave, in tablature, and in rhythm slashes

RHYTHM SLASHES are written above the stave. Strum chords in the rhythm indicated. Round noteheads indicate single notes.

THE MUSICAL STAVE shows pitches and rhythms and is divided by lines into bars. Pitches are named after the first seven letters of the alphabet.

TABLATURE graphically represents the guitar fingerboard. Each horizontal line represents a string, and each number represents a fret.

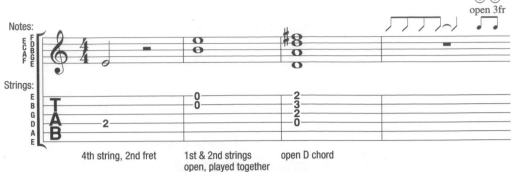

4th string, 2nd fret   1st & 2nd strings open, played together   open D chord

definitions for special guitar notation

SEMI-TONE BEND: Strike the note and bend up a semi-tone (1/2 step).

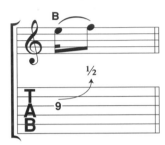

WHOLE-TONE BEND: Strike the note and bend up a whole-tone (whole step).

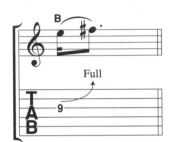

GRACE NOTE BEND: Strike the note and bend as indicated. Play the first note as quickly as possible.

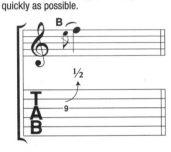

QUARTER-TONE BEND: Strike the note and bend up a 1/4 step.

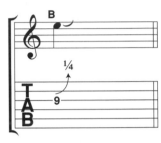

BEND & RELEASE: Strike the note and bend up as indicated, then release back to the original note.

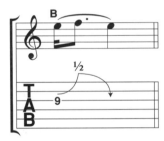

COMPOUND BEND & RELEASE: Strike the note and bend up and down in the rhythm indicated.

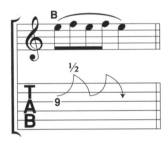

PRE-BEND: Bend the note as indicated, then strike it.

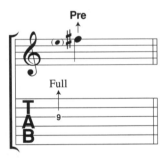

PRE-BEND & RELEASE: Bend the note as indicated. Strike it and release the note back to the original pitch.

UNISON BEND: Strike the two notes simultaneously and bend the lower note up to the pitch of the higher.

BEND & RESTRIKE: Strike the note and bend as indicated then restrike the string where the symbol occurs.

BEND, HOLD AND RELEASE: Same as bend and release but hold the bend for the duration of the tie.

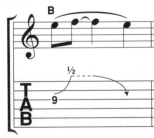

BEND AND TAP: Bend the note as indicated and tap the higher fret while still holding the bend.

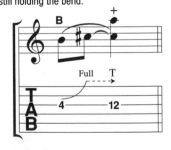

VIBRATO: The string is vibrated by rapidly bending and releasing the note with the fretting hand.

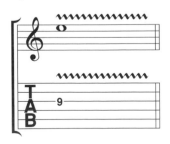

HAMMER-ON: Strike the first (lower) note with one finger, then sound the higher note (on the same string) with another finger by fretting it without picking.

PULL-OFF: Place both fingers on the notes to be sounded, Strike the first note and without picking, pull the finger off to sound the second (lower) note.

LEGATO SLIDE (GLISS): Strike the first note and then slide the same fret-hand finger up or down to the second note. The second note is not struck.

NOTE: The speed of any bend is indicated by the music notation and tempo.

SHIFT SLIDE (GLISS & RESTRIKE): Same as legato slide, except the second note is struck.

TRILL: Very rapidly alternate between the notes indicated by continuously hammering on and pulling off.

TAPPING: Hammer ("tap") the fret indicated with the pick-hand index or middle finger and pull off to the note fretted by the fret hand.

PICK SCRAPE: The edge of the pick is rubbed down (or up) the string, producing a scratchy sound.

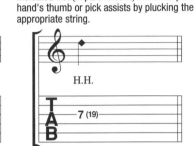

MUFFLED STRINGS: A percussive sound is produced by laying the fret hand across the string(s) without depressing, and striking them with the pick hand.

NATURAL HARMONIC: Strike the note while the fret-hand lightly touches the string directly over the fret indicated.

PINCH HARMONIC: The note is fretted normally and a harmonic is produced by adding the edge of the thumb or the tip of the index finger of the pick hand to the normal pick attack.

HARP HARMONIC: The note is fretted normally and a harmonic is produced by gently resting the pick hand's index finger directly above the indicated fret (in parentheses) while the pick hand's thumb or pick assists by plucking the appropriate string.

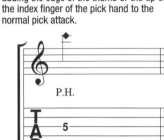

PALM MUTING: The note is partially muted by the pick hand lightly touching the string(s) just before the bridge.

RAKE: Drag the pick across the strings indicated with a single motion.

TREMOLO PICKING: The note is picked as rapidly and continuously as possible.

ARPEGGIATE: Play the notes of the chord indicated by quickly rolling them from bottom to top.

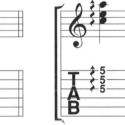

SWEEP PICKING: Rhythmic downstroke and/or upstroke motion across the strings.

VIBRATO DIVE BAR AND RETURN: The pitch of the note or chord is dropped a specific number of steps (in rhythm) then returned to the original pitch.

VIBRATO BAR SCOOP: Depress the bar just before striking the note, then quickly release the bar.

VIBRATO BAR DIP: Strike the note and then immediately drop a specific number of steps, then release back to the original pitch.

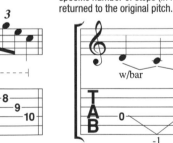

additional musical definitions

 (accent) • Accentuate note (play it louder).

 (accent) • Accentuate note with great intensity.

 (staccato) • Shorten time value of note.

• Downstroke

V • Upstroke

D.%. al Coda

D.C. al Fine

tacet

• Go back to the sign (%), then play until the bar marked *To Coda* ⊕ then skip to the section marked ⊕ *Coda*.

• Go back to the beginning of the song and play until the bar marked *Fine* (end).

• Instrument is silent (drops out).

• Repeat bars between signs.

• When a repeated section has different endings, play the first ending only the first time and the second ending only the second time.

Introduction

Hello, and welcome to ▶▶**Fast*Forward.***

Congratulations on purchasing a product that will improve your playing and provide you with hours of pleasure. All the music in this book has been specially created by professional musicians to give you maximum value and enjoyment.

If you already know how to 'drive' your instrument, but you'd like to do a little customising, you've pulled in at the right place. We'll put you on the fast track to playing the kinds of riffs and patterns that today's professionals rely on.

We'll provide you with a vocabulary of riffs that you can apply in a wide variety of musical situations, with a special emphasis on giving you the techniques that will help you in a band situation.

▶▶**Fast*Forward* Guitar Scales** presents the most important and commonly used guitar scales. In it you can find vital information about pentatonics – the scales behind a huge amount of rock and blues playing. You will learn about the major scale, upon which most Western music is based, and the several types of minor scale. You will also encounter some of the more exotic scales used in music.

All players and bands get their sounds and styles by drawing on the same basic building blocks. With ▶▶**Fast*Forward*** you'll quickly learn these, and then be ready to use them to create your own style.

Guitar Scales

Whatever type of music you play, and whether you play acoustic or electric, it's good to have some knowledge of scales. Knowing your way around a few scales enhances the pleasure of playing the guitar. Scales improve your technique. A few minutes each day running through these patterns will increase the mobility of your fingers. This makes it easier to play any single-note lines – whether solos or melodies – and to change chords if you play rhythm guitar.

Most professionals use scales to warm up their hands before a gig or recording session. If you play lead guitar, then scales are the essential raw material out of which solos are built. A little knowledge of scales can also help you to understand more about keys and chords. Any way you look at it, it's worth knowing about scales.

If you have tried other scale books, prepare to be surprised. This book won't confuse you with loads of numbers so you feel you are trying to play music from a telephone directory. ▶▶**Fast*Forward* Guitar Scales** keeps the emphasis on the *musical effect* of scales. 'What do they sound like?', and 'How and where should I use them?' are the kind of questions this book will answer for you. The book shows how scales work in a range of styles, and in every case the scale is experienced through a piece of music.

Each example in this book is given in musical score, guitar tablature (TAB), and has a corresponding CD track. If you're not too familiar with TAB, it's pretty simple: each number indicates the fret at which the note is played, and each line is a string, going from low to high, i.e. the lowest line on the TAB corresponds to the lowest string on your guitar. Suggestions for fretting fingers are given under the TAB with the scale patterns.

If you find it hard to remember which way up they go, think always of pitch: high notes are above low notes, therefore the highest-sounding string (E) is at the top. Other TAB symbols will be explained as we go along, and there's also a handy reference guide to the most common of these, on pages 4 and 5.

Each musical example is played once with your guitar part, and once without. The first is for you to learn by listening, the second 'play-along' track is for you to practise. There are no backing tracks for the scales themselves.

The examples have a one-bar count-in.

 TRACK 1 tuning notes

▶▶ *JIMI HENDRIX*
You can hear the pentatonic minor in many of his famous solos.

1: The Pentatonic Minor

Our journey into the continent of scales begins with the most popular and commonly used type of scale: the pentatonic scale. Pentatonic literally means 'five notes', and this type of scale is found all over the world. The five black keys on a piano make a pentatonic scale.

This scale is heard extensively in popular music, especially rock and blues. It is a more 'forgiving' scale than some other types. This basically means that it is easier to avoid hitting 'bum' notes in certain musical situations.

A Pentatonic Minor

We will start with the scale that most people first learn on the guitar: the pentatonic minor. We'll play it on A, as this is a popular, guitar-friendly key. The notes are A C D E G. What makes it minor is the distance between the first two notes: three semitones (three frets). In comparison to a major scale, minor scales tend to sound sad.

CD tracks 2 and 3 give you two common patterns for the pentatonic minor. Notice how in the second pattern there is a little shift of position to reach a few higher notes. Make sure you get that second finger at the 9th fret. Remember, the numbers underneath the TAB are fingering suggestions.

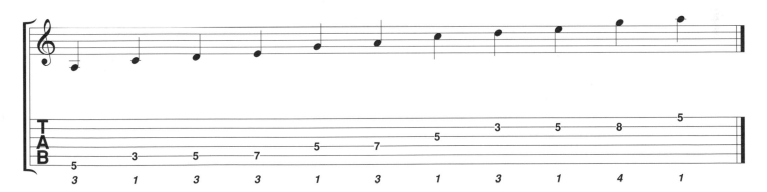

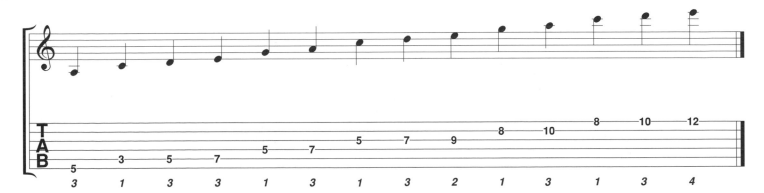

Five Note Rock

In 'Five Note Rock' you can hear the distinctive 'tough' sound of the pentatonic minor played over a rock backing. Whenever you want this hard lead sound play a pentatonic minor over a sequence of major chords. You only have to be careful with this if the chord sequence contains any minor chords.

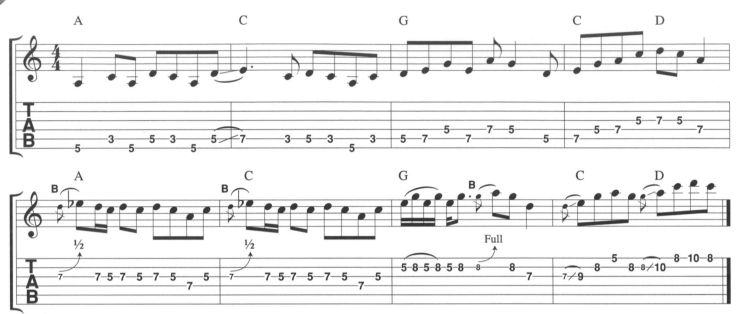

Another trick you can use to enhance your lead playing is to emphasise, in a given phrase, the root note of the chord over which you are playing at that moment. 'Five Note Rock' places an A (first note) against the A chord. Bar two starts with E and C – both of which belong to a C chord, and so on.

The patterns in this book generally have no open strings in them. This means they are *moveable*. If you need to play in a different key, you simply select the right scale for the key and move the pattern *up* or *down* until the starting note is the same as the key note. As long as you play the pattern correctly all the notes will come out right for the new key. For example, if 'Five Note Rock' were in the key of C you would move the pentatonic minor patterns up three frets so they both started on the 8th fret.

FAQ

How do I know which notes to play over which chords?

As long as you have the right scale for the chord sequence it is really up to your sense of melody. Remember, a scale is only the raw material out of which lead phrases, licks and melodies are derived. If you just play up and down a scale pattern it will sound like no more than that – someone playing scales.

Here's a tip for using the pentatonic minor: it can be played over any chord sequence in a minor key or a major key where only the major chords are used.

Five Note Blues

'Five Note Blues' shows how the pentatonic minor scale is used in a 12-bar blues format. The solo uses the pattern at the 5th fret and the little 'extension' box around the 8th. There is only one bend in this passage, in the last bar. In this book, I have deliberately restricted the number of bends in order to give you solos where you can clearly move around scale patterns.

TIP

If you want to work on bends, try
▶▶Fast*Forward* String Bending
(see page 64).

TRACK 6+7

Change Of Ground

Now have a go at 'Change Of Ground'. This also uses the minor pentatonic, but has a very different feel to the previous track. The solo ends with a bar played around the 17th fret. This pattern is the same as that at the fifth, it is just moved up an octave.

 TRACK 8+9

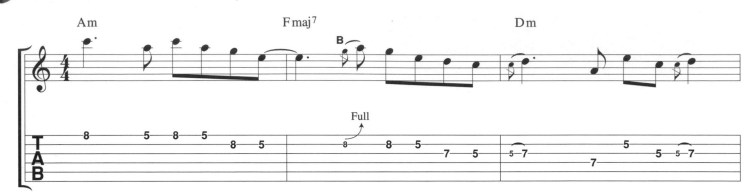

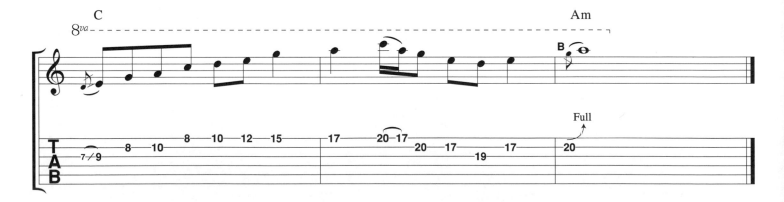

Did you notice how different the feel of the music was? Yet you played notes from the same scale! 'Change Of Ground' teaches you a very important point about scales:

> *The sound of a scale is strongly coloured by the chords over which it is played.*

'Change Of Ground' is in the key of A minor and has two minor chords. As a result, the pentatonic minor scale sounds sadder, and seems to have lost that tough quality you heard in 'Five Note Rock'. The minor key chords bring out the minor sound of the scale.

JOHN LEE HOOKER has been using the E Blues scale for over 60 years!

Three String Ladder

'Three String Ladder' is a 12-bar sequence that introduces the idea of moveable scale shapes. When you're soloing, chances are that you're not going to want to play a scale straight up and down – you want to get some interest into your lead lines! Here's a useful idea for you.

This sequence is in A pentatonic minor again, and the solo is broken up into 'shapes' or three-string patterns. Have a look at the scale shape for the first two bars (shape 1). It uses the 2nd, 3rd and 5th frets only - so you could play those notes in any order, as long as you use the right notes. The same applies to the other shapes. Shape 2 uses notes from the 5th, 7th and 8th frets, shape 3 the 7th to the 10th, and so on.

All the shapes are on the top three strings, but you can transpose these into any key by working out the position of the starting note.

Shape 1

Shape 2

Shape 3

Shape 4

Shape 5

The Blues Scale

We can alter the pentatonic minor to create a new scale, called the 'Blues' scale. This has been used by blues and rock artists such as **Eric Clapton** and **John Lee Hooker**.

In A, the notes of the pentatonic minor are: A C D E G A. By adding the flattened fifth (E♭), we get A C D E♭ E G A. It's a more chromatic-sounding scale, with a 'bluesy' sound.

Here are two patterns for it, with the extra note inserted into the patterns you already know.

TIP

12 is one of the magic numbers that open up the guitar fretboard:

If you move a scale pattern up or down the neck by 12 frets, provided that you don't fall off either end, your notes will have moved an octave higher or lower.

So, the A pentatonic minor scale at the 5th fret, moved up twelve frets to the 17th fret, is the same scale, but an octave higher.

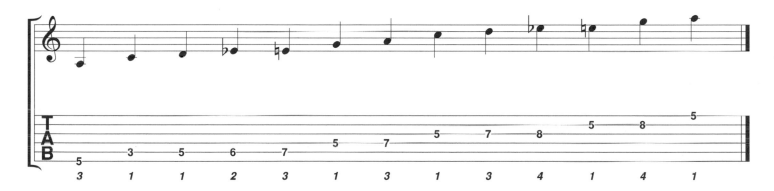

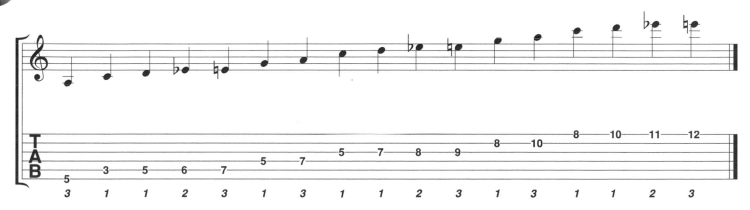

Flat Five Shuffle

Here's another opportunity for you to practise using the Blues scale. In 'Flat Five Shuffle', the new note (E♭) is created by fretting, as in the first four bars, and bending, as in bar 6.

TRACK 14+15

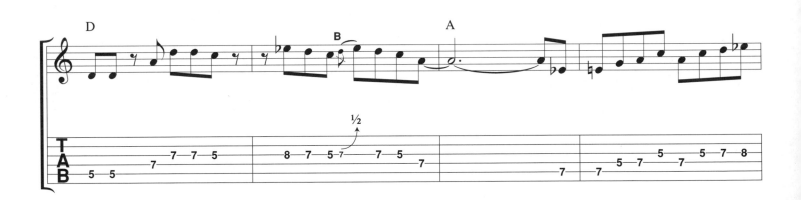

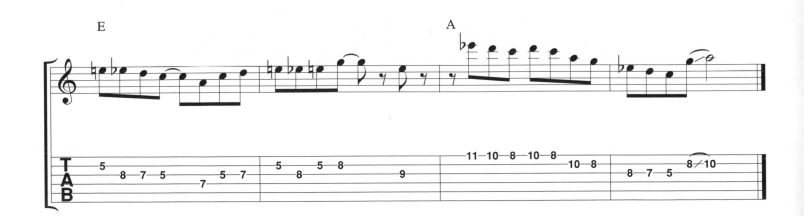

2: The Pentatonic Major

The next most popular form of scale is the pentatonic major, whose notes in A are: A B C# E F#. Here are two examples of the pentatonic major in A. Suggested fingering is underneath.

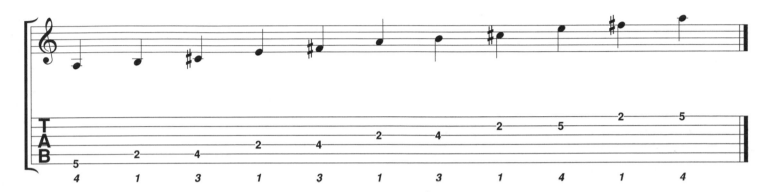

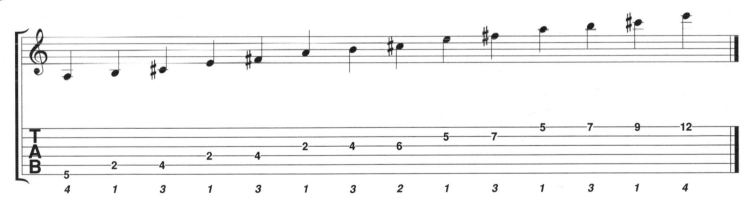

▶▶ ERIC CLAPTON
The pentatonic scale features heavily in Eric's solos, in songs like 'Sunshine Of Your Love', 'Strange Brew', 'White Room' and 'Cocaine'.

Major Five Rocks

Notice that the first three notes are a tone apart. In comparison to a minor scale, major scales seem happy, bright and upbeat, especially if played over major chords. You cannot use this scale in a minor key. If you don't believe me, try playing it over the backing track to 'Change Of Ground' – the results will be hideous! Here's 'Major Five Rocks':

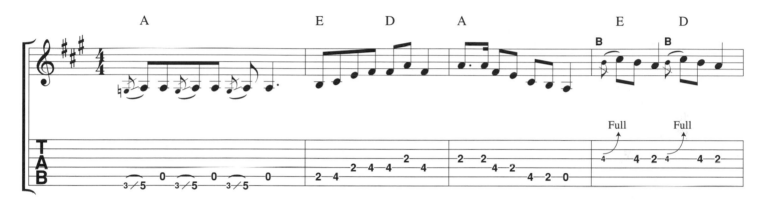

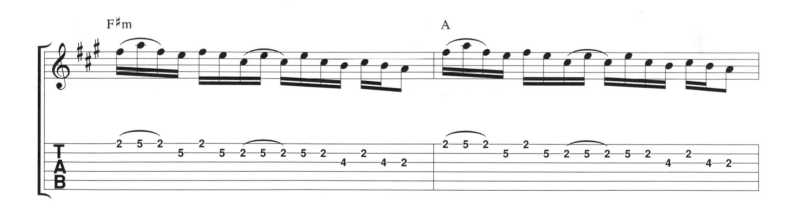

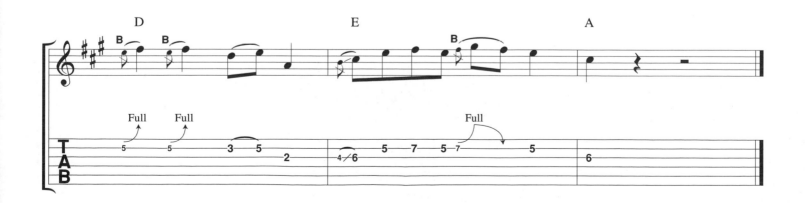

Major Shuffle

'Major Shuffle' starts higher up the neck on the 4th string, before reaching the same pattern as the previous track, an octave higher at the 14th fret (2 +12 = 14). Work these distances out on the fretboard by referring to where your first finger is on a given scale pattern. Listen for the distinctive, buoyant, 'up' feeling generated by the pentatonic major on an up-tempo blues. Bars 1-2 are almost the same as 3-4; there's just a change in fingering.

Twin Lizzy

'Twin Lizzy' shows what the major scale sounds like played over a mixture of major and minor chords in the key of A major. The minor chords bring out a new expressive quality from the scale by the way they 'colour' some of the notes.

This example is written in the style of '70s rock band **Thin Lizzy** who specialised in twin lead guitar. As you play the written part you will hear another guitar playing along with you a little higher. This guitar is panned to one side; your part is more central in the mix.

TRACK 22+23

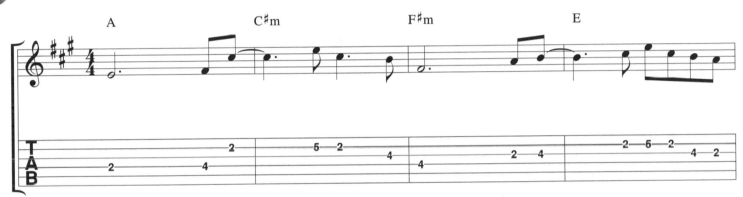

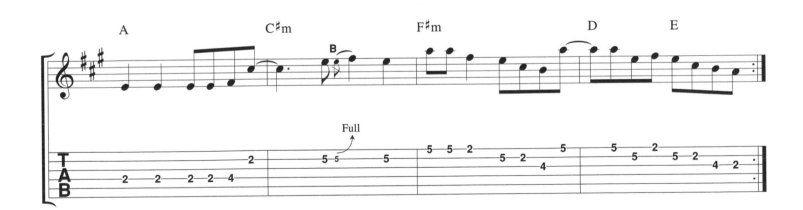

Major Lament

'Major Lament' is a slow, bluesy piece that matches 'Three String Ladder' in providing 'three-string scale shapes' up the neck for the A pentatonic major. The principle is the same:

each pattern is a mini 'solo shape' that you can move around the neck, with five different moveable patterns. Notice how the minor chords colour the major scale notes in a powerful way.

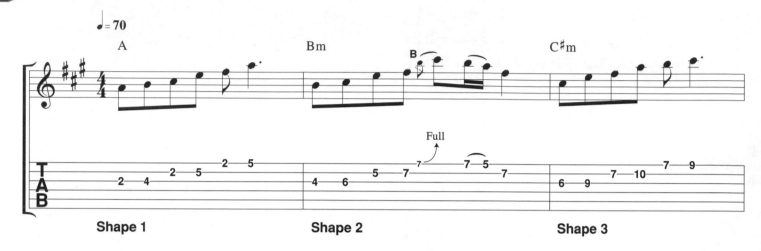

Shape 1   **Shape 2**   **Shape 3**

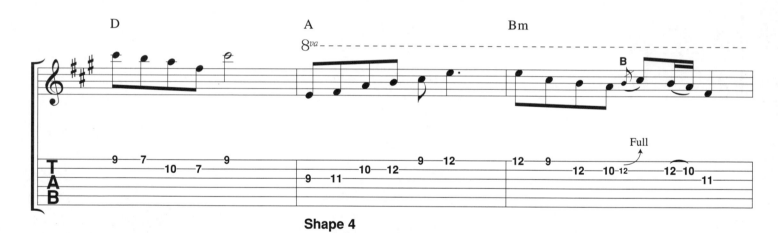

Shape 4

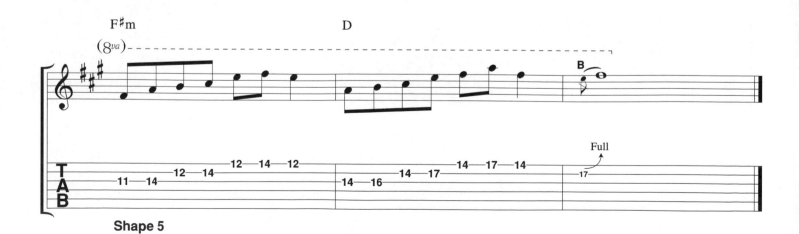

Shape 5

The Major Blues Scale

In the same way that we created the 'blues scale' by altering the pentatonic minor, we can create a 'major blues scale' in A by adding a ♭3 (C) to the pentatonic major: A B C C♯ E F♯ A. This adds an unexpected 'spice' to it. Sometimes the ♭3 is produced by bending and other times by fretting – there's a subtle difference in tone.

TRACK 26

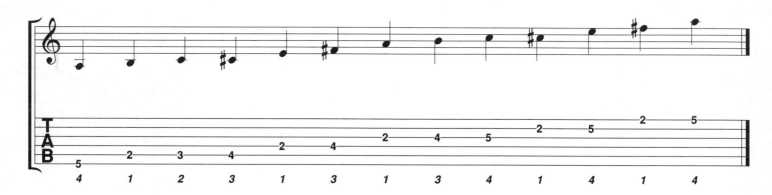

TRACK 27

Major Blues Boogie

'Major Blues Boogie' starts with a riff built on the A major blues scale and then breaks into some lead lines. Notice the effect of the C and C♯ next to each other. In the last couple of bars a two-beat lick is played at different octaves as if the guitar is talking to itself.

 **TRACK 28+29**

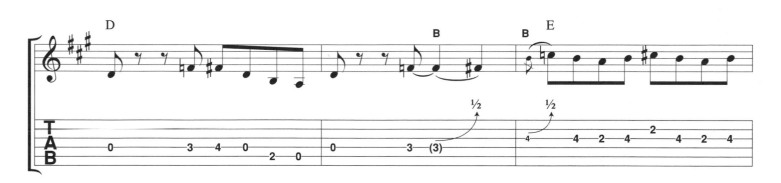

25

3: The Major Scale

After the pentatonic scales, the next most important is the major scale. This scale is the basis for most Western music, whether popular or 'classical'. It consists of seven notes arranged in a sequence of intervals: tone, tone, semitone, tone, tone, tone, semitone. In frets this would be 2-2-1-2-2-2-1.

You can test this for yourself. Hold down any note on any string below the 10th fret (assuming you have a 22-fret electric). Play it, then move up the string according to the 2-2-1-2-2-2-1 pattern, playing each note as you go. What you hear is a major scale.

If we take C as our starting note, the notes for a scale of C major would be C D E F G A B C. The semitone gaps between notes 3 and 4, and 7 and 8, just happen to coincide with E-F and B-C, the two pairs of notes which are a semitone apart.

If we start on any other note, some notes in the scale will need to be lowered or raised to preserve this pattern. Thus, the scale of A major is: A B C♯ D E F♯ G♯ A – where three sharps are needed to get the right 'gaps'.

Here's the scale of A major:

TRACK 30

Tip

This scale is excellent for finger practice. Played regularly with a metronome, these patterns can help increase your speed. Quicken the metronome slowly as you adjust to a given rate of notes per beat.

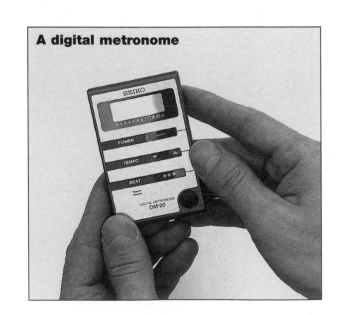

A digital metronome

Pentatonic/Major Scale Table

We can now compare the pentatonics with the
major scale:

	1	2	3	4	5	6	7
A major	A	B	C	D	E	F♯	G♯
A pentatonic major	A	B	C♯		E	F♯	
A pentatonic minor	A		C	D	E		G

From this diagram you can see that all three have
A and E. The pentatonic major is merely an
abbreviated version of the full major, with notes 4
and 7 dropped. The pentatonic minor drops
notes 2 and 6, and flattens the 3 and 7.

A Major (An Octave Higher)

Here's the A major scale one octave higher with
the root note on the 5th string.

Smooth Seven

'Smooth Seven' is in a ballad style and shows the melodic fullness of the major scale over a mixed sequence of chords. The pattern is based around the 5th fret over two octaves, with the root note on the 6th string.

TRACK 32+33

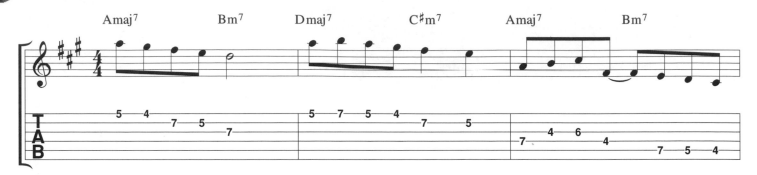

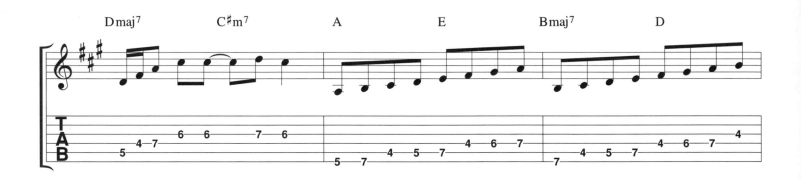

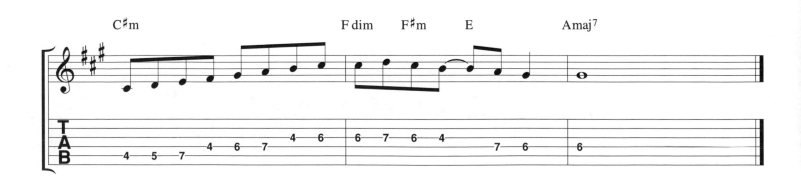

Soulful Seven

'Soulful Seven' is in a soul style and uses a pattern based around the 12th fret, starting on the 5th string. In the previous track, 'Smooth Seven', the root note was on the 6th string. It is always useful with any scale to have one pattern where the root is on the 6th and another where the root is on the 5th, and is therefore higher in pitch. A combination of the two will give plenty of scope for a solo. Try experimenting with these two patterns.

TRACK 34+35

Tip
With root notes on the 6th or 5th string, you have at least two places on the neck to play with any given scale, one higher or lower than the other.

Usually, scales are notated so that each finger takes a fret and the whole pattern keeps within a four-fret 'box', but it is possible to finger a scale so that the fingers span five frets. This is useful when playing above the 12th fret because the frets are smaller. This pattern uses the same notes as the first scale you played (A major), but with different fingering.

TRACK 36

Conversation In A Major

The major scale lends itself to many different musical situations. 'Conversation In A Major' is in a simple jazz style. The track features a 'call–and–answer' guitar part. You will hear the phrase you are meant to play first in the guitar panned to one side – you then answer it, playing where the central, slightly distorted guitar is. The phrases are very short in this piece. In the final bar the two guitars play at the same time.

TRACK 37+38

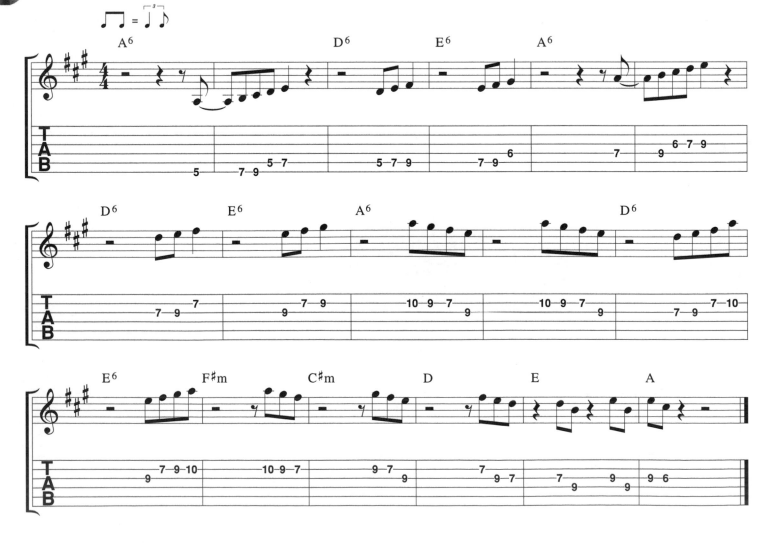

The Bebop Major

Now let's give the major scale a slightly jazzy flavour by adding the flattened 7th. This gives us an eight-note scale popular with jazz musicians in the days of 'bebop'.

Bebop Talking

'Bebop Talking' is another 'call-and-answer' piece. For the first eight bars you play only in the even numbered bars (2, 4 etc). In the odd bars, the first guitar plays a phrase and you echo it exactly in the next bar. In bars 9-10 these echoes start to happen within a single bar – so watch out! For the rest of the piece your part is different to the first guitar, on beats 3 and 4 of each bar.

► JAMES HETFIELD used the E natural minor scale in the Metallica classic 'Nothing Else Matters'.

▶▶ *FastForward*™
Guide To Guitar

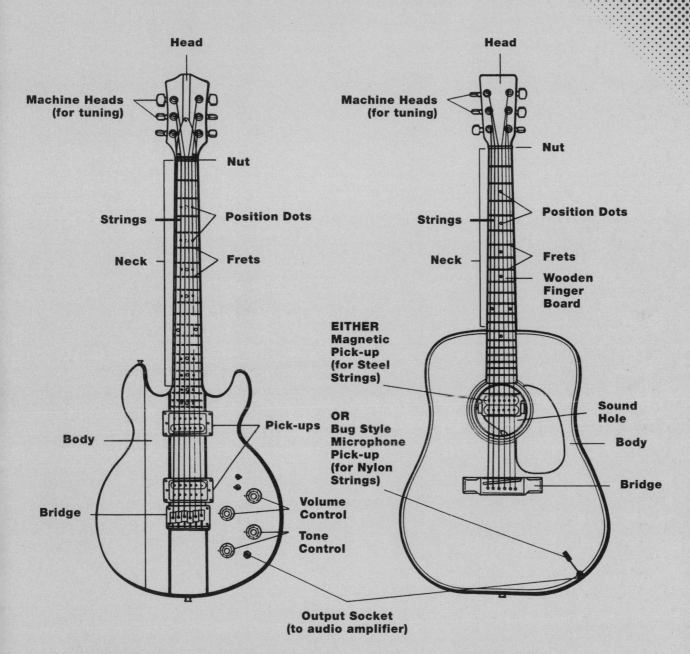

Head

Machine Heads (for tuning)

Nut

Strings

Position Dots

Neck

Frets

Body

Pick-ups

Bridge

EITHER Magnetic Pick-up (for Steel Strings)

OR Bug Style Microphone Pick-up (for Nylon Strings)

Volume Control

Tone Control

Output Socket (to audio amplifier)

Head

Machine Heads (for tuning)

Nut

Strings

Position Dots

Neck

Frets

Wooden Finger Board

Sound Hole

Body

Bridge

The Guitar

Whether you have an acoustic or an electric guitar, the principles of playing are fundamentally the same, and so are most of the features on both instruments.

In order to 'electrify' an acoustic guitar (as in the diagram), a magnetic pick up can be attached to those guitars with steel strings or a 'bug' style microphone pick-up can be attached to guitars with nylon strings.

If in doubt check with your local music shop.

Tuning Your Guitar

Tuning

Accurate tuning of the guitar is essential, and is achieved by winding the machine heads up or down. It is always better to 'tune up' to the correct pitch rather than down.

Therefore, if you find that the pitch of your string is higher (sharper) than the correct pitch, you should 'wind down' below the correct pitch, and then 'tune up' to it.

Relative Tuning

Tuning the guitar to itself without the aid of a pitch pipe or other tuning device.

Other Methods Of Tuning

Pitch pipe
Tuning fork
Dedicated electronic guitar tuner

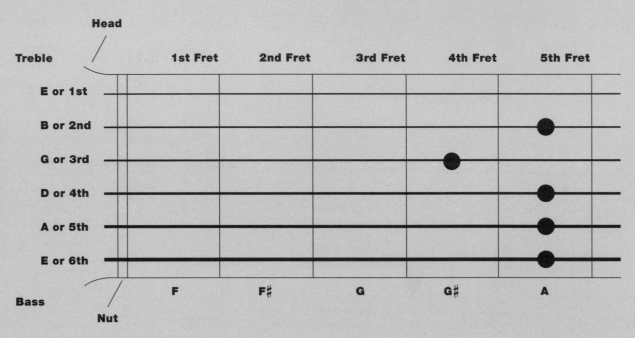

● Press down where indicated, one at a time, following the instructions below.

Estimate the pitch of the 6th string as near as possible to **E** or at least a comfortable pitch (not too high or you might break other strings in tuning up).

Then, while checking the various positions on the above diagram, place a finger from your left hand on:

- The 5th fret of the E or 6th string and **tune the open A** (or 5th string) to the note (A)

- The 5th fret of the A or 5th string and **tune the open D** (or 4th string) to the note (D)

- The 5th fret of the D or 4th string and **tune the open G** (or 3rd string) to the note (G)

- The 4th fret of the G or 3rd string and **tune the open B** (or 2nd string) to the note (B)

- The 5th fret of the B or 2nd string and **tune the open E** (or 1st string) to the note (E)

Chord Boxes

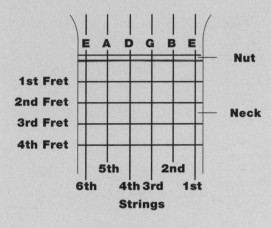

E A D G B E

Nut

1st Fret
2nd Fret
3rd Fret
4th Fret

Neck

5th   2nd
6th 4th 3rd 1st
Strings

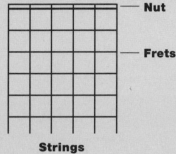

Nut

Frets

Strings

Chord boxes are diagrams of the guitar neck viewed head upwards, face on, as illustrated in the above drawings. The horizontal double line at the top is the nut, the other horizontal lines are the frets. The vertical lines are the strings starting from E or 6th on the left to E or 1st on the right.

Any dots with numbers inside them simply indicate which finger goes where. Any strings marked with an **x** must not be played.

The fingers of your hand are numbered 1, 2, 3, & 4 as in the diagram below.

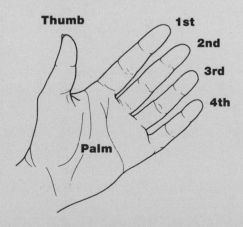

Thumb   1st
              2nd
              3rd
              4th

Palm

The A Chord

6 5 4 3 2 1
Frets
1st
① ② ③
2nd
3rd
4th
5th

x

x = do not play this string

All chords are major chords unless otherwise indicated.

Left Hand
Place all three fingers into position and press down firmly. Keep your thumb around the middle of the back of the neck and directly behind your 1st and 2nd fingers.

Right Hand Thumb Or Plectrum
Slowly play each string, starting with the 5th or A string and moving up to the 1st or E string.

If there is any buzzing, perhaps you need to:-
Position your fingers nearer the metal fret (towards you); or adjust the angle of your hand; or check that the buzz is not elsewhere on the guitar by playing the open strings in the same manner.

Finally, your nails may be too long, in which case you are pressing down at an extreme angle and therefore not firmly enough. Also the pad of one of your fingers may be in the way of the next string for the same reason.

So, cut your nails to a more comfortable length and then try to keep them as near vertical to the fretboard as possible.

Once you have a 'buzz-free' sound, play the chord a few times and then remove your fingers and repeat the exercise until your positioning is right instinctively.

Holding The Guitar

The picture above shows a comfortable position for playing rock or pop guitar

The Right Hand
When STRUMMING (brushing your fingers across the strings), hold your fingers together.

When PICKING (plucking strings individually), hold your wrist further away from the strings than for strumming.

Keep your thumb slightly to the left of your fingers which should be above the three treble strings as shown.

The Plectrum
Many modern guitar players prefer to use a plectrum to strike the strings. Plectrums come in many sizes, shapes and thicknesses and are available from your local music shop.

Start with a fairly large, soft one if possible, with a grip. The photo shows the correct way to hold your plectrum.

The Left Hand
Use your fingertips to press down on the strings in the positions described. Your thumb should be behind your 1st and 2nd fingers pressing on the middle of the back of the neck.

4: The Minor Scales

There is only one type of major scale, but there are *three* types of minor scale. In this section we are going to look at each of them.

The Natural Minor

The most common minor scale for soloing in popular music is the natural minor (also known as the Aeolian Mode - see p.41). In A minor, this would be: A B C D E F G. Notice that no sharps or flats are needed to get the pattern of intervals, which is 2-1-2-2-1-2-2.

However, if you were to use the natural minor in another key, you would have to use sharps or flats to preserve the interval spacing - that's what makes it sound like the natural minor.

We have added two notes – B and F – to the pentatonic minor. These notes can be very expressive, bringing a new dimension to the five we were using.

 **TRACK 42**

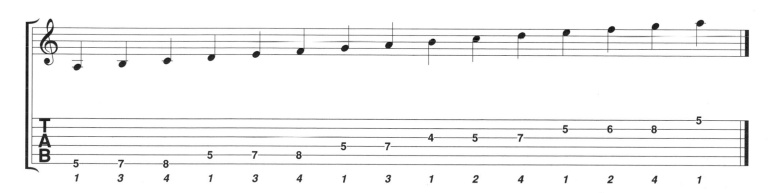

Minor Changes Needed

'Minor Changes Needed' shows how to use the natural minor for a rock solo. The first two bars take you up the scale pattern at the 5th fret.

TRACK 43+44

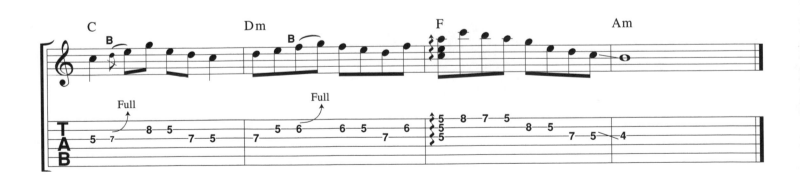

A Natural Minor

Here's the A natural minor scale at the 12th fret, with the root note on the 5th string.

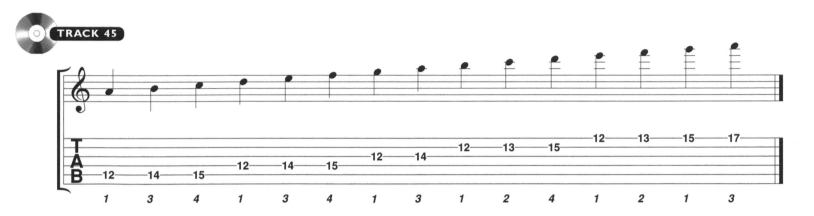

Celtic Blues

'Celtic Blues' is a folk melody in the style of Breton harpist **Alan Stivell**, and guitarist **Dan Ar Bras**. We also have a new time signature: 6/8. Basically, each bar has two main beats, each of which divide into three. The count in consists of 1.. 2.. Notice the 'waltz' feel. The scale pattern is around the 12th fret.

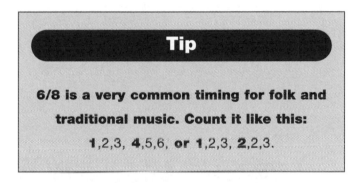

Tip

6/8 is a very common timing for folk and traditional music. Count it like this:

1,2,3, **4**,5,6, **or 1**,2,3, **2**,2,3.

The Harmonic Minor

The second type of minor is called the harmonic. It involves one change from the natural minor: the seventh note is raised by a semitone. This creates a large 1½ tone jump between notes 6 and 7 (F-G♯), which gives the scale an unusual flavour. Here's the scale with the root note on the 6th string, starting at the 5th fret, in A.

12/8 Explained

Each beat divides into four groups of three quaver beats. Basically, count four beats in the bar, but sub-divide each beat by three, e.g:

1,2,3, **2**,2,3, **3**,2,3, **4**,2,3.

Folk Lament

'Folk Lament' is in 12/8 time. That means each beat divides into three. You will see lots of examples of three quavers played on the beat in this example. Much of this piece works from a pattern for A harmonic minor moving off the 5th string at the 12th fret.

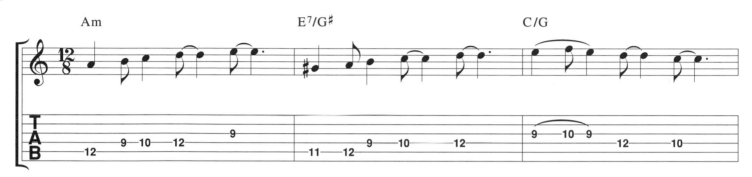

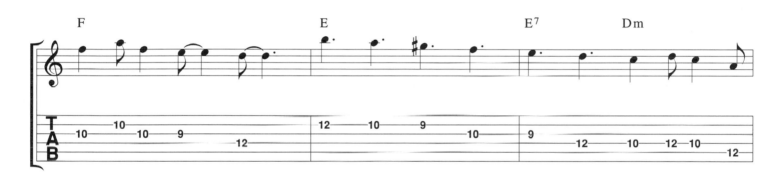

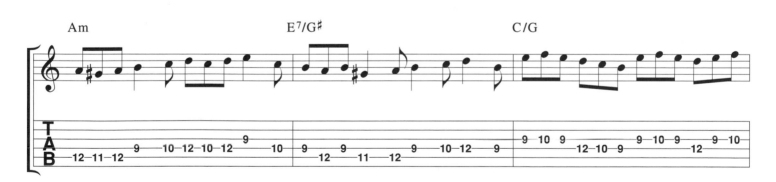

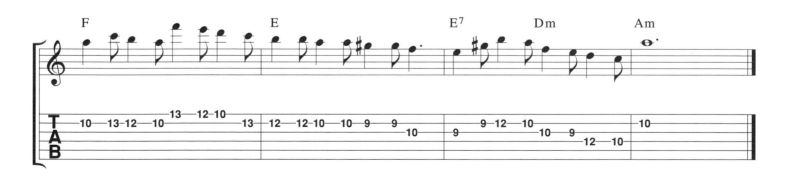

A Touch Of The Heavies

In rock, the harmonic minor is exploited either for a neo-classical effect, or for an 'Eastern' sound. 'A Touch Of The Heavies' uses the scale for a riff. Notice the F-G♯ interval, especially in bar 10, and how that interval creates the exotic sound if it is used correctly.

TRACK 51+52

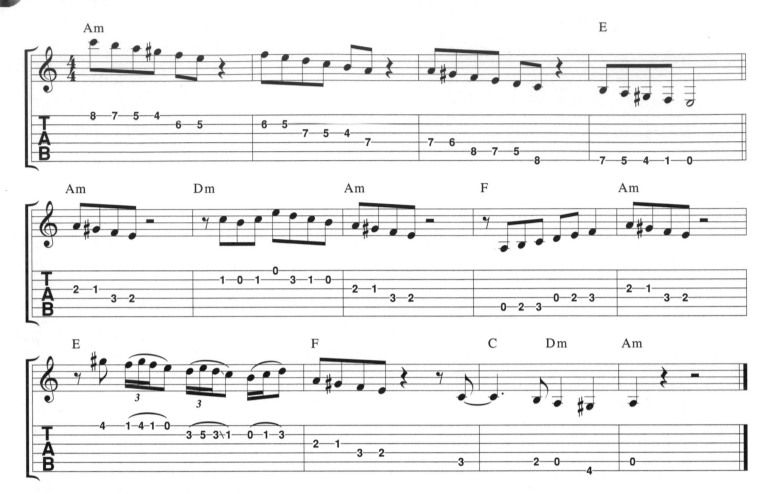

The Melodic Minor

The third, and most unusual minor scale type is the melodic minor. It got its name from the fact that it removes the awkward jump between the sixth and seventh notes in the harmonic, which is difficult for singers.

Here's the nasty bit: ascending, the harmonic goes A B C D E F♯ G♯ A but on the way down, it *changes* by removing the sharps (A G F etc.). This scale is not used much in popular music, you'll be relieved to hear!

TRACK 53

Sheer Madness

Because it uses different notes descending from the notes it uses ascending, this scale is almost impossible to use in improvisation or composition, and is very rare in popular and rock music.

However, I've managed to write one example for you to try, based on the 'white reggae'/'ska' style of popular '80s chart act **Madness.**

Let's compare the minor scales to each other:

Minor Scale Table

	1	2	3	4	5	6	7
A pentatonic minor	A		C	D	E		G
A natural minor	A	B	C	D	E	F	G
A harmonic minor	A	B	C	D	E	F	G♯
A melodic minor	A	B	C	D	E	F(♯)	G(♯)

CRISPIAN MILLS
Kula Shaker might not have had a career without their heavily-borrowed Jimmy Page licks – all from the mixolydian mode, of course.

5: The Modes

Having covered pentatonics, major, and three types of minor scales, let's now have a go at another group of scales collectively known as *modes*. There are seven main modes and these date from Ancient Greece (which is a long time before **Elvis**!). They have been used by composers and folk musicians in Western music for centuries, though some rock guitarists talk as if they dug them up in the 1980s! Modes are simply scales that use a different pattern of intervals to the scales you have already played. Here they are, with the intervals marked underneath (in semitones, or frets):

Modes Table

	1		2		3		4		5		6		7		8
Ionian	C	2	D	2	E	1	F	2	G	2	A	2	B	1	C
Dorian	D	2	E	1	F	2	G	2	A	2	B	1	C	2	D
Phrygrian	E	1	F	2	G	2	A	2	B	1	C	2	D	2	E
Lydian	F	2	G	2	A	2	B	1	C	2	D	2	E	1	F
Mixolydian	G	2	A	2	B	1	C	2	D	2	E	1	F	2	G
Aeolian	A	2	B	1	C	2	D	2	E	1	F	2	G	2	A
Locrian	B	1	C	2	D	2	E	1	F	2	G	2	A	2	B

Tip

Modes are designed to be played without needing to use sharps or flats – however, they can be transposed into any key simply by using the patterns of tones and semitones.

Notice anything about the Ionian? It's the major scale. And the Aeolian? That's the natural minor. So you already know two of the seven modes. That leaves us five more to try.

All The Modes On A

Each mode has a different interval pattern, so any mode can begin on any note as long as sharps and flats are used to make all the gaps fit the right sequence shown above.

To illustrate this point, here is a table showing all the modes transposed to start on the note A:

Modes Table (On A)

Mode name	Notes, with tone/semitone pattern underneath								Easy Name
A Ionian	A	B	C♯	D	E	F♯	G♯	A	Major Scale
	2	2	1	2	2	2	1		
A Dorian	A	B	C	D	E	F♯	G	A	Natural minor + ♯6
	2	1	2	2	2	1	2		
A Phrygrian	A	B♭	C	D	E	F	G	A	Natural minor + ♭2
	1	2	2	2	1	2	2		
A Lydian	A	B	C♯	D♯	E	F♯	G♯	A	Major Scale + ♯4
	2	2	2	1	2	2	1		
A Mixolydian	A	B	C♯	D	E	F♯	G	A	Major Scale + ♭7
	2	2	1	2	2	1	2		
A Aeolian	A	B	C	D	E	F	G	A	Natural Minor
	2	1	2	2	1	2	2		
A Locrian	A	B♭	C	D	E♭	F	G	A	Natural minor + ♭2 + ♭5
	1	2	2	1	2	2	2		

Notice that various flats or sharps appear on some of these modes but the interval patterns are identical to the previous diagram. Some books suggest that you learn new scale patterns for each mode. However, an easier way of approaching this is to just work out which notes need to be altered from either the major scale or the natural minor (see 'Easy name' in the table above).

Now, what can we do musically with the five modes that we have not yet played?

The Blues/Rock Scale (Mixolydian)

Let's take the Mixolydian first. You can think of this scale as being similar to a major scale but with the 7th note flattened by a semitone.

Since blues music uses lots of flattened 7ths this is a common effect.

TRACK 56

Here Come Ol' Flat Seven

It is easy to introduce this scale into your playing. Simply take any major scale pattern, locate the 7th notes and move them back a semitone. It is often found in '50s rock n roll, so here's 'Here

Come Ol' Flat Seven' in the style of **Chuck Berry** to get you going. Allow for the extra 3 beats on the count-in.

TRACK 57+58

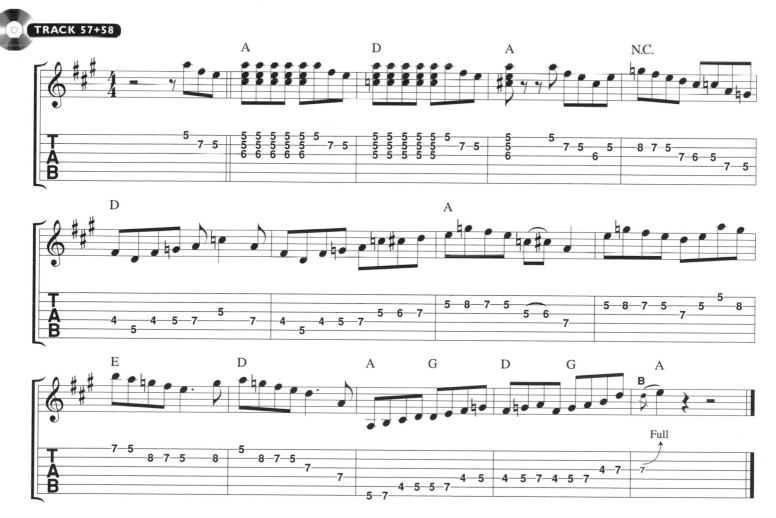

The Speed Metal Scale (Lydian)

The Lydian mode is also quite similar to a major
scale, but with the fourth note sharpened.

 TRACK 59

Raise Four Rock

The Lydian mode was quite popular in speed
metal and similar late 1980s guitar styles.

'Raise Four Rock' is in that style but not quite so
fast! Notice that it has quite an unsettling effect.

TRACK 60+61

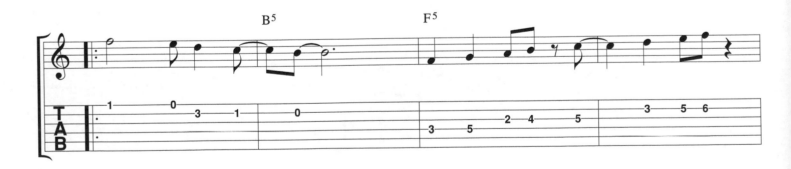

Lydian Surprise

By subtly introducing the Lydian note into the harmony we can give ourselves an opportunity to use the Lydian mode in a more melodic way.

'Lydian Surprise' is in the key of F major, which normally has a B flat in the scale (F G A B♭ C D E F). This means that the chords G and Cmaj7 (both of which contain a B natural) would not normally occur in this key.

However, the Lydian mode on F uses the notes: F G A B C D E F. So where the G and Cmaj7 chords occur it is necessary to avoid hitting a B♭. Using the F Lydian mode instead provides the right notes.

TRACK 62+63

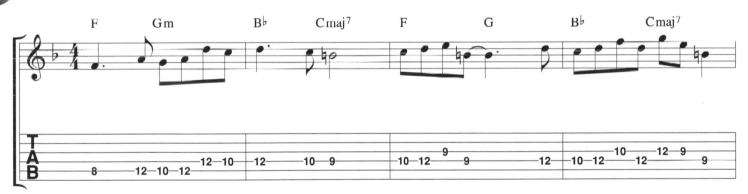

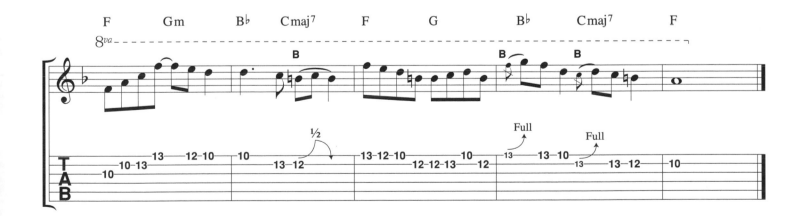

The Latin /Folk Scale (Dorian)

Two of the modes can be likened to the natural minor scale (itself a mode, as we have just seen). Let's take the Dorian first. A Dorian is: A B C D E F♯ G – the only difference is that the sixth note is sharpened. This gives the Dorian a slightly more 'angular', tense quality. The sharpened sixth is not quite as 'depressed' as the sixth found on the natural minor scale.

TRACK 64

For Carlos

'For Carlos' is a short example of the Dorian mode in the Latin-American style of **Santana.** The Dorian mode suits the Am-D chord change, but would not suit an Am-Dm change. If you see a chord sequence with Am-Dm-Em you need the natural minor; if the chords are Am-Dm-E the harmonic minor will be useful, and if you see an Am-D change it's the Dorian you want.

TRACK 65+66

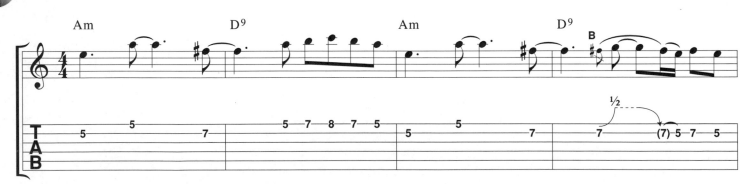

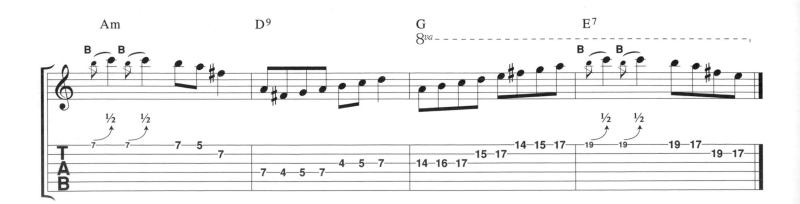

Dorian Groove

'Dorian Groove' gives a sense of the tension the Dorian mode can give because the whole solo is played over just the Am chord.

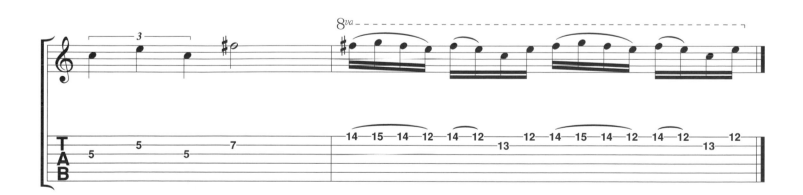

The Spanish Scale (Phrygian)

The other mode which has a minor affinity is the
Phrygian, which in A is: A B♭ C D E F G. You
can think of this as the natural minor with a
flattened 2nd. It has a distinctive Spanish sound,
and is heard in much flamenco music.

TRACK 69

Phrygian Western

'Phrygian Western' could be from a film
soundtrack. The effect on the main guitar part is
tremolo, which gives a shimmering quality to the
note. To take advantage of the guitar's open strings
this piece is in E Phrygian (E F G A B C D).

Also, notice the unusual time signature of 7/4
which produces a long and assymetrical rhythmic
pulse. However, the count-in on the CD is still
four beats.

TRACK 70+71

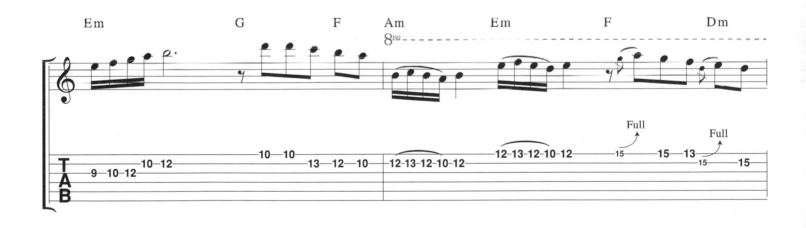

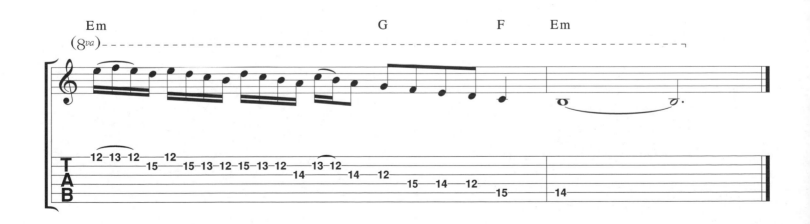

The Odd One Out (Locrian)

The 'odd man out' among the modes is the Locrian. This is because it is neither really major or minor inclined but diminished.

A Locrian is A B♭ C D E♭ F G – like the natural minor with a flattened 2nd *and* 5th.

TRACK 72

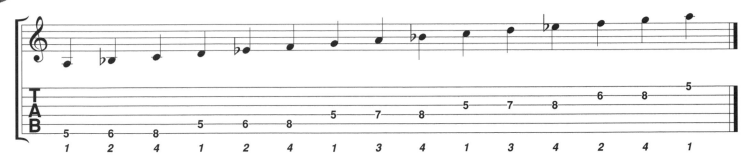

Take A Dim View

Of all the scales we have looked at, this is the first where there is not a perfect fifth (3½ tones) between the 1st note and the 5th. All of the other modes on A include the note E (the 5th).

This makes the Locrian mode quite unsettling, as 'Take A Dim View' shows. Listen out for the diminished 7 chord in bars 7-8:

TRACK 73+74

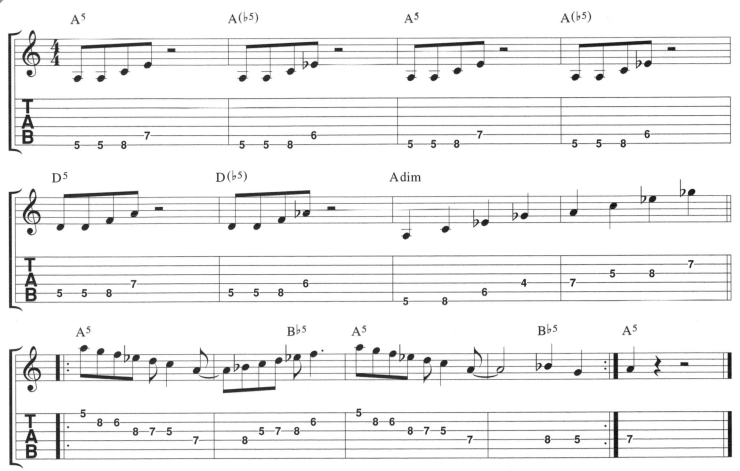

6: Unusual Scales

In this final section we will play a selection of more unusual scales. These are scales which will only sound good in certain musical situations. You won't be able to just solo over a 12-bar blues or a 16-bar rock phrase with these. Their successful use will depend on musical context – in other words, what does the song sound like? What chords are there? Are there any serious clashes of notes?

The Whole Tone Scale

The first few scales in this section play around with the interval gaps. All the modes we have looked at so far have resulted from a mixture of 1 and 2 fret gaps (semitones and tones). The whole tone scale is based on the idea of creating a scale entirely from tones. The result (on A) is: A B C♯ D♯ E♯ F G (the G is actually F double sharp, but we won't worry about that technicality!). It starts off like the major scale and then deviates at the 4th note along, and it ends with a whole tone – like the Mixolydian. Notice it has only six notes, not seven.

TRACK 75

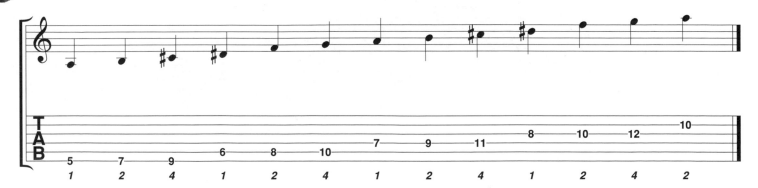

'The Whole Truth'

The whole tone scale has an open, slightly ambiguous sound. It has been used in jazz and other types of improvisational music where melody is more important than harmony. 'The Whole Truth' is an example of its ambiguous sound:

TRACK 76+77

WES MONTGOMERY knows a thing or two about chromatic scalic lines.

The Chromatic Scale

If you can make a scale out of whole tones, why not try all semitones? If we play all the semitones between A and the A an octave above it we have a 'chromatic' scale (meaning 'colour').

 TRACK 78

Fully Chromatic

Chromatic scales are great for finger exercises. It is rare to find them in music, but chromatic passing notes are often used to add more interest to a piece. These are defined as notes which are not part of the scale on which the music is based. In A major the notes A♯/B♭, C, D♯/E♭, F, and G are all chromatic because they are not part of the major scale. Chromatic passing notes can be slipped in to link other notes – it's all a matter of taste and timing. They are a central device in jazz playing. Let's try 'Fully Chromatic':

 TRACK 79+80

The Diminished Scale

Another odd scale with a 'fixed' interval sequence is the diminished scale, which goes 2-1-2-1-2-1- 2-1, i.e. alternating tones and semitones. In A this produces: A B C D E♭ F G♭ G♯.

A Little Jazz After Dark

This is useful for playing over a diminished 7th chord such as A diminished: A C E♭ G♭, or any other combination of these notes. Diminished 7th chords are mostly found in jazz and progressive rock but occasionally crop up in blues (as in 'Need Your Love So Bad') and popular songs of the 1930s and 1940s. As with the whole tone and chromatic scales, you would not normally play a whole solo on the scale. 'A Little Jazz After Dark' demonstrates the jazz flavour of this scale:

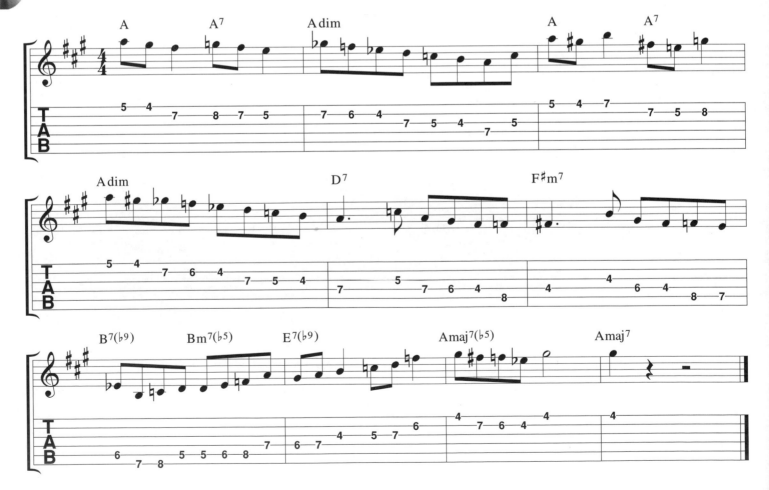

The Kumoi Scale

Early on in the book we played major and minor pentatonics. There are many other types of pentatonic scale, used around the world.

Here is one exotic example, the kumoi scale from Japan, which is: A B♭ D E F (if transposed onto A).

TRACK 84

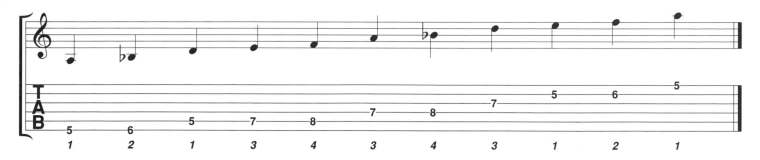

Beware The Volcano

Knowing scales such as this can be useful if you want to create music which evokes another country. 'Beware The Volcano' alludes to one of

James Bond's oriental adventures. The kumoi scale is transposed onto E here: E F A B C.

TRACK 85+86

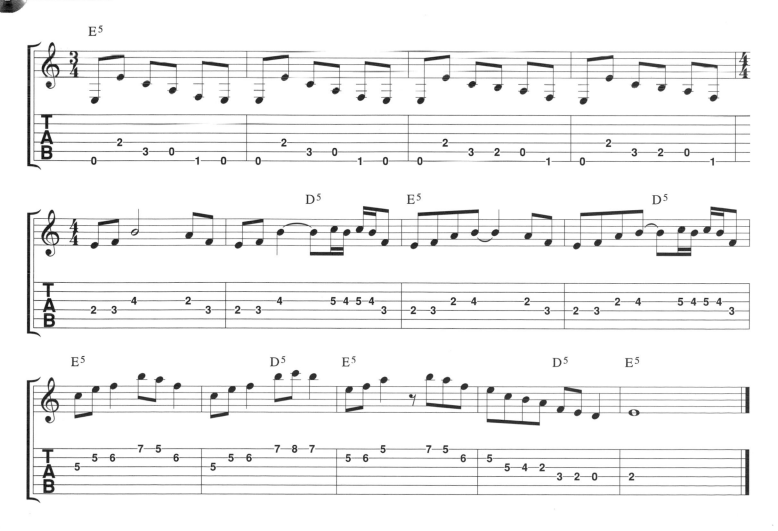

The Byzantine Scale

Earlier we looked at the harmonic minor scale
and the opportunity it gives for an exotic sound.
Here's a scale that will do the job even better –
the Byzantine scale, which, transposed to A, is A
B♭ C♯ D E F G♯ A. If you compare this with D
harmonic minor you can see the similarity:

A Byzantine	A	B♭	C♯	D	E	F	G♯	A		
D Harmonic Minor				D	E	F	G♯	A	B♭	C♯

The Byzantine scale has sharpened the fourth
note of the harmonic minor. It has not one, but
two of the 1½ gaps which characterise the
harmonic minor.

Byzantine Splendour

'Byzantine Splendour' shows what you can do
with this both in terms of heavy riffs and rock
lead. Clever use of bends will make it sound even
more exotic.

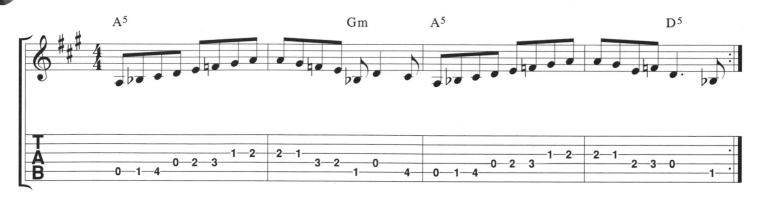

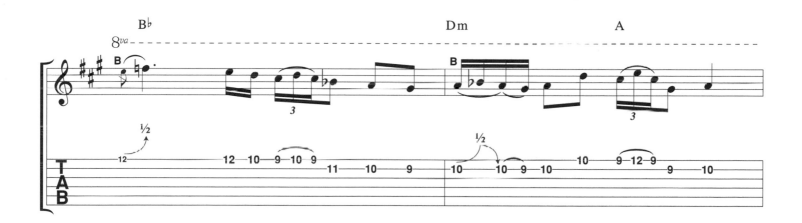

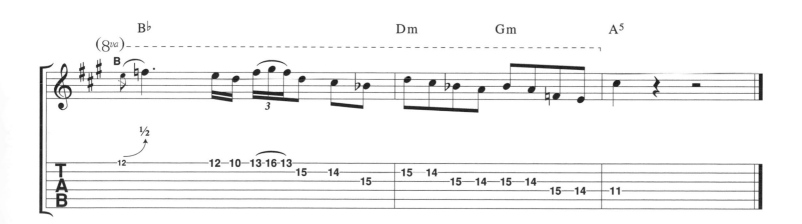

Get More Out Of Your Scales!

To finish, here's two examples that show how you
can sometimes get more out of what you already
know. We've already played a bebop scale where
the flattened 7th is added to the major scale.
Here's a variant with an added flattened 6th (F):
A B C♯ D E F F♯ G♯ A.

Rendezvous

You can feel the jazz influence of this extra note
in 'Rendezvous'. Cappuccino at the ready!

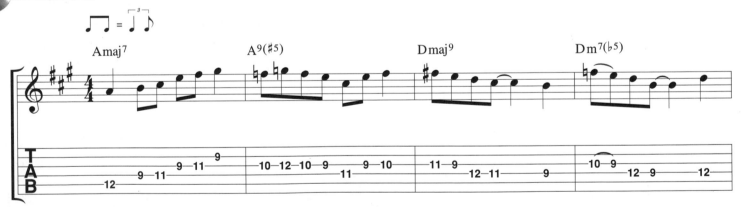

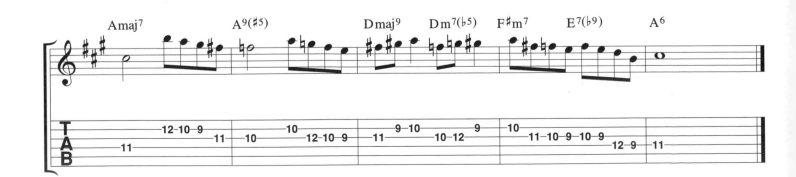

Extended Pentatonic

Finally, here's a neat way of re-using a pentatonic. Imagine you are soloing over a progression in the key of A major. The obvious pentatonic to use is A pentatonic major (A B C# E F#). However, what about moving this pattern up four frets? You will then be playing C# pentatonic minor, but still using some of the same notes in the A major scale. Compare these using the table below:

A Major	A	B	C#	D	E	F#	G#	A	B
A Pentatonic Major	A	B	C#		E	F#			
C# Pentatonic Minor			C#		E	F#	G#		B

It works because you are playing notes 2, 3, 5, 6, and 7. But the odd thing about it is that you never land on the key note A, which gives this combination an odd, 'hollow' effect.

You can do the same thing by playing B pentatonic minor two frets lower. There, you end up only playing notes 1, 2, 4, 5, and 6. The sound is slightly different.

Where's The Route?

The last example 'Where's The Route?' features this 'mediant pentatonic' (the third note of the scale is called the mediant) as you can hear in some of **Marc Bolan**'s guitar solos on **T.Rex** albums like *The Slider* and *Tanx*. I'm sure he never stopped to figure out why it worked – he just liked the sound. Maybe you will discover some of your own tricks by experimenting. Why not try different scales over some of the backing tracks featured on this CD?

TRACK 93+94

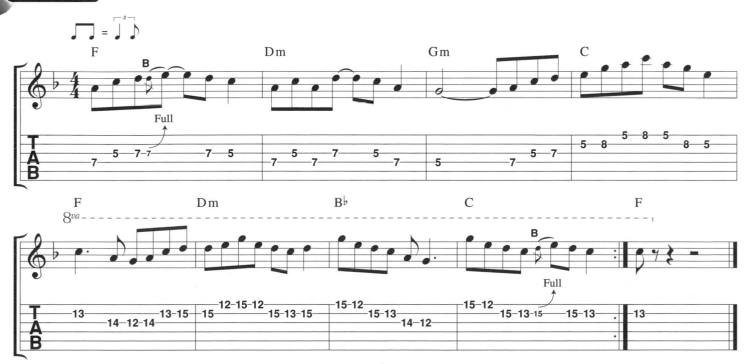

▶▶ **ROBBEN FORD** even made up his own scale (minor pentatonic major 6th), an alternative to the straight minor pentatonic. (But HE says he borrowed it from B.B. King – how about that for pedigree!)

Scale Tips And Tricks

▶▶ Use a metronome! It's the best way to improve your speed, and also helps you to play evenly.

▶▶ When you're practising your scales, always start slowly and try to build up speed. You should aim to play the scale at around 180 notes per minute, but to start with, you should aim for half this speed.

▶▶ Don't just stick to one playing position. After all, you won't be doing that when you're soloing! Try ascending using one position, then descend using another, or shift position halfway through a scale.

▶▶ Don't just go up and down the scale, or you'll never be able to use it in a solo. Try using arpeggios and some of the exercises featured here to build melodic lines that you can use.

▶▶ Always use your ears as well as theoretical knowledge when you are working out which scale will fit over a given chord progression.

▶▶ Don't attempt to fit a new scale over every chord. Check out the key, work out which chords belong in the key, and usually a straight major, minor or pentatonic will do the job.

▶▶ If there are any chords which are not in key, break them down into their constituent notes and see what foreign notes they contain. Then you might be able to think of a scale which will have them – or you could just avoid hitting those notes at that moment.

▶▶ Another good trick for breaking up monotony is to just play the notes of any odd chord as an arpeggio, temporarily abandoning scale movement.

▶▶ Finally, practise a little every day, and try to start building in scales each time you practise. If you haven't been able to solo before, you'll find it starts to come naturally!

Further Reading

If you've enjoyed this book, why not check out some of the books shown below, available from all good music retailers or bookshops, or in case of difficulty, Music Sales Limited (see page 4). You can also visit our website: **www.musicsales.com**.

FastForward: Slide Guitar
AM958903

Learn how to use the bottleneck, altered tunings, string-damping and vibrato, and play in the style of Elmore James, Muddy Waters and Ry Cooder.

FastForward: Altered Guitar Tunings
AM958914

Discover the power of altered tunings to change your guitar sound. Improve your strumming, fingerpicking, rhythm guitar and bottleneck playing, in the styles of Joni Mitchell, Robert Johnson, James Taylor and Keith Richards.

FastForward: String Bending
AM958947

String bending is an essential technique for most popular styles of guitar music. This book will show you everything you need to know to play professional sounding riffs and solos used by all the famous players of blues, rock, folk and soul.

FastForward: Alternative Rock Guitar
AM958530

A complete history of alternative rock over the last four decades. Steer away from mainstream rock, and learn exactly what gave bands like Television, The Jam, The Smiths, The Stone Roses, R.E.M., U2, Nirvana and Radiohead their unique sounds.

Chord Chemistry
AM942580

We've all watched someone play and wondered 'What's that chord? It sounds great!' This book shows you how to create those great-sounding chords and sequences. Find out how to spice up basic repertoire, work on your strumming, and learn how to use 'add', 'sus', 7ths, 9ths and partial chords, and how to mix slash, root, pedal and barre chords into your sequences.

Chord Chemistry Songbook
AM952930

18 all-time great songs specially chosen to help you build your chord skills, including: 'Hey Joe', 'Happy Xmas (War Is Over)', 'Wonderwall', 'I Got You (I Feel Good)', and 'How Deep Is Your Love'.